The Busy, Lively, Sleepy, and Quiet Pond

by Kim Borland

illustrationed by Bradley Clarke

Editorial Offices: Glenview, Illinois • Parsippany, New Jersey • New York, New York
Sales Offices: Needham, Massachusetts • Duluth, Georgia • Glenview, Illinois
Coppell, Texas • Ontario, California • Mesa, Arizona

The pond looks sleepy and quiet. Not much happens here. Or does it?

Take a closer look. Plants grow. Insects hum and buzz. Animals swim, fly, and hop. There is life near the water all year long. The pond is full of life! What's the word for the pond in spring? Busy!

3

Warm spring rain and melting snow fill the pond. Pond water is fresh, not salty like the ocean.

Trees begin to bud. Fruits and berries begin to grow. Flowers get a little taller every day.

In the spring, frogs and turtles dig out of their muddy winter homes on the bottom of the pond. The animals swim, eat, and lay eggs.

Ducks, geese, and birds build nests for their eggs. Soon the pond will be busy with animals and their young!

Hot summer days warm the water.
A mother duck and ducklings swim in
the pond. They look under the water for
food. Frogs sit on lily pads. They catch
bugs with their long sticky tongues.

6

In the summer, the turtle eggs hatch. The baby turtles run toward the water.

The ducklings were born a few months ago. Now they learn to fly in circles above the pond.

What's the word for the pond in summer? Lively!

In the fall, the days grow cooler. The leaves on the trees change color. The ducks and geese fly away to warmer places. Turtles rest in the sun. Soon they will go deep under the mud at the bottom of the pond.

What's the word for the pond in fall? Sleepy!

The beavers work to repair their home, called a *lodge*. They add branches, logs, and mud to the lodge.

The beavers also gather food for the winter. They store food in the lodge and under the water. The beavers will have enough food for the whole winter.

Beavers store tree bark, roots, shoots, and water plants underwater to last the winter.

The winter days are cold. The ducks and geese are gone. The frogs and turtles sleep in the mud at the bottom of the pond.

The top of the pond turns to ice. Some animals live here all year long. They look for grass, seeds, and fruits around the pond.

The cold winter winds blow. Snow drifts across the pond. Tracks show that some animals visit the pond in the winter.

What's the word for the pond in winter? Quiet.

In a few months, it will be the spring again. The ice will melt, and the animals will return. Once again, the pond will be a busy, lively place!

Spring

Summer

Fall

Winter